GOD BLESS
You

[signature]

ISAIAH
40:31

Anthony Ritthaler

Soaring
With
Eagles

A Book Of Freedom, Strength and Power

PUBLISHED by PARABLES
Earthly Stories with a Heavenly Meaning

ANTHONY RITTHALER

Pathways To The Past

Each volume stands alone as an Individual Book
Each volume stands together with others
to enhance the value of your collection

Build your Personal, Pastoral or Church Library
Pathways To The Past contains an ever-expanding list of
Christendom's most influencial authors

Augustine of Hippo
Athanasius
E. M. Bounds
John Bunyan
Brother Lawrence
Jessie Penn-Lewis
Bernard of Clairvaux
Andrew Murray
Watchman Nee
Arthur W. Pink
Hannah Whitall Smith
R. A. Torrey
A. W. Tozer
Jean-Pierre de Caussade
Thomas Watson
And many, many more.

Title: Soaring with Eagles
Anthony Ritthaler
Rights: All Rights Reserved
ISBN 978-1-945698-12-5
Doctrinal theology, Inspiration
Salvation, Meditation
Other books by this author include: Walking On The Water With Jesus (Volume 1 and 2) and A Devil From The Beginning.

Anthony Ritthaler

Soaring
With
Eagles

A Book Of Freedom, Strength and Power

PUBLISHED by PARABLES
Earthly Stories with a Heavenly Meaning

ANTHONY RITTHALER

Tony's Words Of Freedom, Strength and Power

"The Devil is a liar,
but an Eagle just flies higher."

"When danger is all around
the Eagle takes off to higher ground."

"We have a choice as Christians:
we can hang with the crows, or soar with the pros."

"Your finest hour will always be
when you soar with God's Power."

"Fly with the Lord in Power, Strength, and Glory
and never allow Satan to write your life's story."

"When others around you complain and cry,
be mature take off and fly."

"Whenever you soar with God
this world will think your odd."

"When you are fighting the World, the flesh, and the
Devil allow the Holy Spirit to move you
to a higher level."

"The greatest person in life is not he who obtains the most,
but it is he who is controlled by the blessed Holy Ghost."

"If you desire to be rare,
that's when God can take you anywhere."

"Those who have the touch from on High
will always give Satan a black eye."

"An Eagle often flies alone,
but his journey leads to Gods Throne."

"When you're facing all the Demons of Hell,
just fly to God and sing it is well."

"When like the Eagle you soar to the mountain, God
will allow you to drink from His fountain."

"When an Eagle takes flight he never looks back, but
that won't stop the Pharisees from taking smack."

Table of Contents

Tony's Words Of Freedom, Strength and Power
Special Thanks
Introduction
1. God's Power on Full Display
2. Angels Among Us
3. Good Things Come to Those Who Wait
4. Prayer is Always the Answer
5. Peace be Still
6. The Highway to Hell
7. Jesus is Always Right on Time
8. Sheltered in the Arms of Jesus
9. Soaring with Eagles

10. I Put off the Old Coat and Put on the New
11. A Blissful Moment in Time
12. Hiding under the Shadows of the Almighty
13. All Things are Possible with God
14. Red and Yellow, Black and White, Their All Precious in His Sight
15. The Importance of Waiting on God
16. Jesus Knows Exactly What He is Doing
17. Surely Goodness and Mercy Shall follow Me All the Days of My Life
18. Love Conquers All
Conclusion

Special Thanks

There are five preachers in particular that I want to thank for their influence upon this book. Without their help through the years there is no way on earth this book would be possible. A big thank you goes out to Dr. Lawrence Mendez for his impact on my life. Without your preaching sir I would not be where I am today. Thank you Dr. Kidd for teaching me how to walk with the Lord; your impact on my life has been humbling. Thanks Evangelist Larry Bell for teaching me integrity through the life you live. Brother you are a rock sir and I love you so much in the Lord.

A very special thank you goes out to Evangelist Todd Hicks for always being there for me. My friend you have been a great encouragement and I'm honored to know you. Last but not least I want to thank my dear Pastor Timothy Ammon for his dedication over the years. Pastor I've learned a great deal through your ministry and it's a joy to serve at Hope Baptist Church.

Thanks to everyone else that also helped me along this road. I love you all so very much.

With Love
Bro Tony

INTRODUCTION

Welcome to my brand new project called, "Soaring with Eagles" I'm honored you would take time to read this book. I'm confident that you will not be disappointed. Each inspirational story has been coated with prayer with the conviction that this book will lift you to greater heights with God. This book will be a blessing and an encouragement to anyone searching for a deeper walk with the Master.

There are a variety of powerful, unique stories that will bless folks from all walks of life. As you read this project I'm confident that the Spirit of Almighty God will challenge you, bless you and cause you to hunger for power with God. Every story in this book has one ultimate purpose: to bring glory to the risen Lamb. Soaring with Eagles will encourage pastors, equip saints, and convict the sinner.

May Gods blessed Holy Spirit do a work in each and every life that takes time to dive into this book. Soaring with Eagles is meant for all Christians not just a select few. God wants us all to soar to heights not yet discovered and this book will give you the tools to make that happen.

My prayer is that thousands who live in fear and dismay will raise up out of there depressed state and will soar to God with complete confidence that Christ loves them and longs to use them like never before.

Enjoy the book everyone and soar for His honor and for His Glory all the days of your life.

Phillipians 4:13 "I can do all things through Christ which strengtheneth me."

Chapter One

God's Power on Full Display

Throughout history there have been countless warriors of the faith who have seen and done wonders through a spirit filled life. Men and women, who have ignored the skeptics and have accomplished marvelous things through the power of a higher source. Men like Charles Finney: he once saw 50,000 people saved in one week; or women like Fanny Crosby who was used by God to touch millions of lives through her beautiful hymns.

In days of old many Christians could move mountains through the strength of their prayer lives. Today, unfortunately, these stories are rare: and it's all due to how people live.

Hebrews 13:8 says," Jesus Christ is the same yesterday, today, and forever." The Bible clearly tells us that God never changes, and He never will. Sadly it's us who have changed and we have no one to blame but ourselves for the lack of miracles we see on a daily basis. Please allow the following story to minister to you and fire you back up for God again.

A few years ago, God in heaven opened up a door for my family and allowed us to move from a condo in Canton, Michigan to a house in Romulus, Michigan. To watch God work throughout the moving process was humbling in every way. Quickly, after we moved in, we discovered that a new roof was needed. We had about 6,000 dollars left over from the move so I contacted a man I knew about putting a new roof on for us. The man's name was Miguel and he, along with his whole family, agreed to do our roof for just over 5,000 dollars. The labor took around 5 days and we were amazed by the work he and his family did. Miguel notified me that he ran out of daylight to put on the sealer that would prevent water from getting under our roof but Monday after work He would complete it for us.

Monday came and as we were working we received horrible news and it came suddenly. The news report said rain is coming and it's coming fast so be ready. When we heard the news Miguel immediately left to go put the sealer on but on his way to my house rain pounded the area. Once I personally heard the news I quickly begged the Lord to keep my roof safe and God heard my feeble cry.

My dear mother happened to be over that day and she had a front row seat to one of the greatest miracles she ever witnessed. She told me over the phone that it was raining everywhere around her except in our yard. My mom said rain was pounding every house around her but God refused to allow the rain to come inside our fence. For over 40 minutes this took place and she said it looked like a hand was holding it back. God proved His power that day and through His grace our roof was spared.

We serve a God of wonders and a God who wants to display His power like in days gone by. What we saw that day left many speechless and we will remember this story forever. Folks, nothing is too hard for God and the clouds are nothing more than the dust of His feet.

Chapter 2

Angels Among Us

Whether people choose to believe it or not I'm telling you by the authenticity of the Word of God angels are among us. The Bible is loaded with accounts from the Old Testament and the New Testament of angels appearing suddenly with a message from the Lord.

Personally I know of five times in my life where God sent an angel along my pathway and so many could give the same testimony. If God would open our spiritual eyes we would stand in amazement by how many angels were standing nearby. The Bible says in II Kings 6:17 that Elisha prayed for God to open a young man's eyes and when He did the mountain was full of horses and chariots of fire. Angels are among us folks and that's why it's so important to live right. You see, most people who see angels walk with God. The following story was a blessing to me and I pray it will be a blessing to you.

One Saturday night as I was preparing my Sunday morning lesson verses started dancing through my mind about the subject of angels. Within thirty minutes I had over 100 verses written down about angels and around ten stories of folks that met them from people I know. Power filled my house and peace filled my heart as I wrote down the title of my message, "Angels among us." The very next morning as we were traveling to the church the Spirit of God was present and I could not wait to teach this little lesson. I remember walking into the building and being approached by one of my teens and her glow was amazing. Before anyone else arrived that morning she began to tell me all about her week and the angel she meet. The story she gave me was incredible and it was very detailed. After hearing her story I had no doubt in my mind that God had sent an angel her way to simply encourage her. After she gave me this story the bus arrived and a few more teens joined us for the message. A young women came that morning. I had never seen her before, and, imagine this -- out of all the names she could of had it was the name, Angelica. She told me after class that day that something told her to come to church that morning so she came. Angelica was never there before and she has never come back but she came that day. The Power of God was with us that morning and all the teens were weeping after they heard this message.

My friends, angels are very much among us and I venture to say you have come across a few in your day, Psalms 34:7 says this, "The angel of the Lord encampeth round about them that fear Him, and delivereth them."

Keep your eyes open my friends for you never know when one is nearby.

Chapter 3

Good Things Come to Those Who Wait

The Word of God is full of stories that express the great benefits of waiting on God. Psalms 15:4 says, "For whatsoever things were written aforetime were written for our learning, that we through patience and comfort of the scriptures might have hope." God led men to pen down these stories so that generations to come could learn how to conduct their lives properly. Perhaps the greatest story about waiting on God and enjoying its benefits is the story about Abraham and Isaac. We all understand that Abraham was a man of great faith; who trusted God every step of the way. Time after time throughout his life God tested his faith by bringing trials into his life. Each test was passed with flying colors and each trial brought him closer to the Lord.

One day God appeared to Abraham and told him that even though he was to old to produce offspring Abraham would! He was destined by God to become a father again and his elderly wife Sarah would bring forth the promised seed. Although Abraham did not understand how this could happen he trusted God for 25 years and never gave up. At 90 years of age Sarah gave birth and Abraham became the father of Isaac. God called Abraham a friend of God, a term He never gave anyone else and it's all due to Abraham's faith in God. How many of us would have doubted God and thrown in the towel before 25 years had passed?

Many people lose out on God's blessings because they grow weary of waiting on God. The Bible still teaches that "all things work together for good to them that love God, to them who are called according to his purpose." Sometimes God will bring instant answers to prayer; but not always. We pray and our prayers are answered according to His timing. Everything will work out according to His will. We must learn how to lean on Him for every need rather than ourselves. God has a plan and purpose for everything that happens. If you're going through a trial please understand that God has a reason for it. The more you trust God the greater your life will turn out. This next story will prove that good things come to those who wait and who pray.

The Word of God tells us in Psalms 37:4 to "delight thyself also in the Lord; and He shall give thee desires of thine heart." Personally I cling to this promise daily along with many other promises from God's Word. We serve a gracious and loving God who desires to bless us through the course of our lives. I believe that when we love God and serve others God will be sure to reward us with desires we have as well. My dear wife is a music teacher and she does not ask for much at all. One day she came to me with two requests to pray over. She said, "I've always wanted a piano so I can practice at home and teach my children music. I also would like a curio cabinet to store my different little items in." My response to my dear wife was that we will make this a matter of prayer and trust God for as long as it takes. Around one year later we received a call from Erin's mother that was a blessing beyond measure. Through this phone call it was made known to us that a dear lady in Hillsdale, Michigan felt led to give us a piano. She told my wife that she wanted to give her the piano to be a blessing to our family. Shortly after this conversation ended our telephone rang again and this time it was my wife's best friend Megan on the other line. Megan said, "Erin, do you have any room for a curio cabinet I want to give it to you. Folks, after waiting a whole year for God's direction He saw fit to bless us with both gifts within the same hour.

Chapter 4

Prayer Is Always The Answer

What ever happened to people who could get a hold of God without much struggle? Let me ask another question. Whatever happened to people who lived with clean hands, clean minds, and clean hearts?

In these last days finding this combination in people is like finding a needle in a haystack. Christians today have filthy, darkened hearts, and dirty minds. Psalms 66:18 clearly states, "If I regard iniquity in my heart the Lord will not hear me." Christians all over this country spend most of their time trying to impress people and they don't even care about pleasing God. Christians in this day and age fill their lives with busy schedules and they forget all about God. Men of God who mounted the pulpits 200 years ago lived clean lives and prayed for hours every day and it' brought revival. Today preachers are too busy to pray and it shows through their preaching. Revival seems to be a thing of the past and that's because members and pastors have become lazy in the work of God. The Bible teaches over and over again that Gods power is available to those who hunger and thirst after righteousness. We need a whole army of people with passion again who care more about pleasing God than they do pleasing themselves.

The following story demonstrates the importance of having a clean life before God. People depend on us to pray for them and if we are away from God they will walk away empty. Allow this story to help you live a holy life.

A dear man from my work came to me broke and crying one day and I could tell he needed help. This man did not attend church but he was always a blessing to me so I wanted to be a blessing to him. This man quickly asked for money and I quickly said I'm broke but God is not. We bowed our heads right there and I said a quick prayer. My exact words were, "Lord this man has been a blessing to me, please help him in Jesus name amen." I'm glad to report that night after work a woman knocked on this man's door with a check for 2,500 dollars. God will not work through an unclean vessel and it's essential to others that we are effective prayer warriors. Ask yourself right now: when is the last time I know that God heard and answered my prayer? If it's been a while come clean with the Lord today? Souls of men and women hang in the balance.

CHAPTER 5

PEACE BE STILL

It's amazing to me that the worst storm the disciples ever encountered was calmed by just three words, "PEACE BE STILL". When Jesus is close by fear melts away by the sweet sound of His voice. Millions of people all around this universe run to doctors, shrinks, and educated people when trouble arises and those same people leave empty and void of help. Jesus is willing and waiting to help us but most will make Him their last option. There is great power in the name of Jesus Christ and if we have any sense about us we will run to His loving arms when tragedy strikes. The Word of God says in Psalms 34:19,"Many are the afflictions of the righteous but the Lord delivereth out of them all". No matter what storm we find ourselves in we can find deliverance through just three words from the Master "PEACE BE STILL" Allow God to speak to your heart through this next story.

One afternoon, while waiting for my food at McDonalds, I struck up a conversation with a dear woman and her young daughter. The conversation was going well and God's

Spirit was convicting their hearts. As we were speaking I remember looking over to my right and seeing that young daughter start shaking and foaming at the mouth. I quickly turned to the mother and asked what was going on and she said a seizure and this is a big one. People began to rush to her aid to help but I knew we serve the greatest doctor of all. I quickly stepped back and uttered three words, "peace be still". When I said those words that young girl stopped shaking and her body calmed completely down instantly. Her dear mother sat her down so that she could recover. As I went to leave that young girl looked my way and smiled.

Why do we have so much fear when Jesus is near? Stop going to earthly counselors when troubles come! Go to the only one who can calm you spirit - the Lord Jesus Christ. Amen and Amen.

Chapter 6

The Highway to Hell

 The greatest tool the devil uses in destroying people is wicked, ungodly music. The devil uses his music to influence and pollute the minds of untold millions. God's music will always bring joy, peace and contentment. The devil's music will preach pain, rebellion and misery. Many of the famous rock and roll singers willingly admit that they worship Satan. Nothing will cause people to slide towards hell's flames faster than wicked music. Every time I hear rock and roll in public it grieves my spirit and it makes me very uneasy.

 There have been thousands of murders, suicides and fatal decisions caused by people who were under the influence of rock and roll music. Every teen I've ever known who has listened to this music over the years has paid a high price. Once this music enters someone's brain, the chains of bondage will enter into their souls and the devil will enter into their life. The devil will use his music to steal every ounce of joy and power from that person's life. Don't fall prey to the devil. If you listen to this junk get rid of it as fast as you can.

The following story was such a blessing to me because it shut the devil up for a little while. May God bless you through this simple story.

Around four years ago I was at work having one of those stressful, tiresome days and I could not wait to go home. My head was hurting and my body was worn out. I can remember looking at the clock and noticing we only had about an hour left. Moments later a man came in and started blasting a song on the radio called, "Highway to Hell." The absolute last thing I needed at that time was to hear that song so I prayed that God would turn that nonsense off for me. Seconds later the bay door of the shop opened and the wind that rushed in messed with the signal and static filled the air. Three people tried to fix the radio but they could not do it. Finally a man got frustrated and unplugged the radio for good. The rest of the day was peaceful and I'm thankful God answered that prayer.

Why would anyone allow the devil to flood their mind with that trash? If I were you I would leave the devil where he is standing and I would run to Jesus and never look back. Thank God for the victory we have in Christ Jesus.

Please throw the devils music in the trash and replace it with songs that honor God.

If you do, I promise you can leave the highway to hell and you can travel on the highway to heaven.

Chapter 7

Jesus is Always Right on Time

The account of Jesus raising Lazarus from the dead has blessed me my entire life. When others were wondering why Jesus was taking so long, Jesus knew what He was doing and the timing was absolutely perfect. Jesus should never be doubted by fallen man and if He made a promise from His Word it will come to pass. Jesus promised to never leave us nor forsake us and to supply our every need. We, as Christians, doubt God's Word so often and it really affect's our lives. We must understand through life we will have many ups and downs but we will never be alone in this journey. We must trust God at all times and believe that He is working on our behalf. Jesus knows the beginning from the end and if we can't trust Him then who can we trust? Jesus is working behind the scenes of your life and just because you can't see Him it does not mean He is not there. Let me share a story that will help us realize the beauty of God's perfect timing.

Not long ago we fell on hard times and we were concerned

about finances. We had no idea how God would provide. We just knew that He would. During challenging times the devil works overtime to discourage us and cause us to doubt God. My wife asked me how will we get the money to pay our bills. I had no answer. I just knew God would take care of it. Minutes later I received a check in the mail for $554.10. The timing was perfect and we gave God the glory. Shortly after this happened more money came in and it was for $94.79. After the second check came in I looked at my wife and said, "Honey, God has everything under control and His timing is always perfect."

All around the world, on a daily basis, God in heaven does things of this nature for His children. We serve a great God who loves and cares for us. It's high time we stop doubting the Lord and start trusting His every move in our lives. God will never fail us one time.

Chapter 8

Sheltered in the Arms of Jesus

The Word of God teaches in Matthew 18:10 that every child has a guardian angel watching over them. So many people around this world could stand up and tell stories of how their children were heading into danger and something kept them safe. There is an unseen hand of love that hovers around children all around this earth. Personally I've seen this with my daughter numerous times and my wife and I have stood in amazement by all the times God has shown mercy on her. There has always been a special relationship between Jesus and children and that relationship will never change. Jesus loves to reach down and hold children in His arms and He sends His angels to shelter them from many dangerous situations. There are a lot of stories I can give on this subject that would bless your heart but I will just give you one to prove Matthew 18:10 is true.

A few months ago my family and I took a trip to Hillsdale, Michigan to spend time with friends and family. The weather was awesome that week and the fellowship was a blessing as well. My daughter fell in love with the four-wheeler that week and we had a blast driving that thing around. On the last day of our stay in Hillsdale my daughter Hope wanted to ride the four-wheeler one last time so we jumped on and took one final ride. We drove to many different places, up and down hills, around the property and eventually we ended up in a corn field. My daughter said, "Daddy go faster, go faster, so I said, "Hold on tight and we will." We started going very fast and I underestimated how much land we had left and I was running out of room to stop safely. My only option was to slam on the brakes and when I did my precious daughter went flying off the four-wheeler. When she landed on the ground it was like she landed on a pillow and there was no doubt an angel was close by. I quickly parked the four-wheeler and asked Hope if she was O.K. She looked at me and said, "I'm O.K. daddy; let's ride again." Anything could have happened that day especially at the speed we were going but God showed mercy on us that day.

Isn't it wonderful how Jesus shelters children? No man or woman can explain moments like this but we just know it happens. Thank God for a merciful and loving God.

Chapter 9

Soaring with Eagles

The chapter that you are about to read will make the hairs on the back of your neck stand up. I'm confident that this chapter will stand out in your mind as one of the most powerful stories you have ever read. For three solid weeks the Lord over shadowed me and the details of this story will amaze you. Even when I look back at this story now, I still stand in awe by what God did throughout the course of these three weeks. There is no possible way with human tongue I could properly explain every single event that took place but with the help of God I will do my best. Please give me your undivided attention as we travel through a three week period that was totally ordained by God. May God's power fall upon you while you read this story.

One day as my three year old daughter and I were walking through Cracker Barrel I saw something that caught my eye. The moment I laid my eyes upon it I knew, without a shadow of a doubt, I wanted to get it for a preacher friend of mine. What my daughter and I saw that day was amazing to behold and very unique. The item was a four foot statue of an eagle sitting on top of the Liberty Bell and it was a limited edition. Once I decided to get this statue I pulled my daughter close to me and we both prayed for it right there in the store with everyone looking at us. Our prayer to the Lord was full of faith and we asked Him to send the money quickly. Two days later while driving up the road at 2:45 PM God gave me peace that our prayer had been heard. When I arrived home that day I looked in the mail box and there were two checks waiting there for me. One check was for 873 dollars and the other check was for 94 dollars. After receiving these checks we went to the bank and cashed them and went straight back to the Cracked Barrel and bought that eagle statue. We took the statue to my parent's house and stored it there for the night and they loved it as well. On my drive home that night I remember God dealing with me stronger than He ever had before about teaching a lesson called, "Soaring with Eagles". All that night the Lord dealt with me about it and when the morning light hit I had total peace about teaching it the following Sunday morning. The moment I publicly announced I was teaching on the subject, "Soaring with Eagles" God's power struck me like never before – it was awesome! Immediately after this happened I sent a text to a woman and told her what I was teaching and I said, "never in my life had I felt God so strongly." As these words left my mouth a horn beeped from the distance and a truck pulled up for me to unload at work. When it got closer I noticed the company name and out of all the names it could have been it was the Allied Eagle Company. We unloaded 837 items from the truck and every item had an eagle on it. Moments later I received a call from a man I hadn't heard from in a while and he had amazing news. The man on the other line said, "Tony, I'm working at a new golf course right now and I want you to know that anytime you want to golf for the rest of your life you can for free." I responded by saying wow sir, what coarse is this? He responded back and said, "EAGLE CREST," Tony. Out of all the golf courses it could have been it was the one with the word Eagle in it.

All throughout the remainder of that week leading up to Sunday there were eagles at literally every place I went. We knocked on eleven doors that Saturday and every single house had something with eagles on it. In one week we had seen over 1,500 items with eagles on them. Every move we made and every step we took that week was directed by God Almighty.

Sunday finally arrived and I was fired up to preach. We brought that big eagle statue into the services and recorded the message that morning. God moved in a mighty way and four teens were born again. To describe the power we all felt that day is impossible and so many lives were changed. After the service concluded God started dealing with my heart to preach a volume two of this message, because more needed to be helped. I'll never forget after the service a man took us to I-Hops and God was still dealing with me. At I-Hops they give you a name of someone famous from the past and when it's your time to eat they call you by that name to your table. Out of all the names we could have received that Sunday we received Mr. Glen Frey , the lead singer of the musical group called - The Eagles. On the way to Hillsdale, Michigan the following day I asked the Lord to make it clear if He wanted me to teach a volume two of this message. At the moment I had this thought I looked and I saw a seventy-five foot eagle balloon starting back at me and I surrendered to God's will right then and there.

All through out that next week as well eagles were everywhere and so was God's presence. When Sunday arrived we preached, "Soaring with Eagles - Volume two" and a wind from another world swept through that place. A young man from our church was kind enough to record both messages so I asked him to turn it into a video for me. The young man agreed and what happened next is staggering. The very next morning this young man was walking with his boss with my messages in his hand and from out of nowhere a real live eagle landed at his feet. This young man said the eagle was older and it stared at him for what seemed like an eternity before it flew off. He also said his boss was shaking and he stood in amazement that day. The following Saturday, the preacher I wanted to give that statue too was in town, so I went to see him and brought the eagle statue with me. The preacher loved the statue and we took a picture together. After this took place a guest preacher stood up and this is what he said," Folks I do not know why but tonight God changed my message and I want to preach a message called "Soaring with Eagles." I'm telling you God moved across that church and we saw five saved that night.

At the end of these three powerful weeks, on the final day of these amazing events, God did one last thing that put a stamp of approval on it all. As I was driving home on a Monday morning from work it felt like God grabbed my steering wheel and led me in a different direction. I felt like the Lord was driving the car and he led me to a gas station. When I got out of the car I could not believe my eyes. At the Arab owned gas station there was a four foot tall eagle statue on top of the Liberty Bell with an American flag sticking out of it. When I saw that eagle statue I thanked God for the powerful three weeks He allowed me to experience.

So many other things happened in those three weeks that I did not include in this chapter but I assure you they were all from God. All in all, we had seen over 2,000 items with eagles on them in three weeks. Never in my life have I sensed such power as I did for that time period and I will never forget it till the day I die.

In closing this chapter I want to quote Isaiah 40:31. "But they that wait upon the Lord shall renew their strength; they shall mount up with wings as eagles; they shall run, and not be weary; and they shall walk, and not faint."

Chapter 10

I Put Off the Old Coat and Put On the New

    Whenever a person makes their way towards Jesus Christ and accepts His free gift of salvation, automatically he goes from rags to riches spiritually. When we are born we inherit a sinful nature, but when we are born again we receive a brand new nature. In the book of II Corinthians 5:17 Jesus tells us that if any man be in Christ he is a new creature, old things are passed away; behold all things are become new. Although we cannot see it with the natural eye salvation brings instant change from God. At the moment of conversion God takes off are old, filthy, stinky rags and puts on a new, clean and fresh garment of righteousness. Isaiah 64:6 says, "all our righteousness' are as filthy rags." But Psalms 103:12 declares that our sins are "forever removed and forgotten" when we are washed in the blood. It is a spiritual cleansing that sticks with you forever. Salvation brings a sudden change and a new standing with God. We are no longer vile and wretched in the sight of God but instead we are justified and pure through the sacrifice of Christ. Salvation is the greatest thing that can ever happen to you and if you have it you ought to tell others about it. An old black preacher once said, "When I got born the first time momma told me about it, but when I got born the second time I told momma about it." When you match the dingy, old, dirty coat up against God's new amazing coat there is no comparison. Thank God for His love, mercy and compassion. We are so unworthy. For the rest of this chapter I will share with you a story from my past that fits this chapter perfectly. People enjoy this story and it is a good picture of His mercy on us. Allow God to bless your heart with this story.

Many years ago as we were serving God in the city of Detroit God granted me a special blessing one night. My mother had been telling me that it was time to get a new suit because all of my suits were either dated, worn out or old. At that time I was sending all my money to help the church in Detroit; and, I felt guilty about the idea of buying myself a suit. I told my mom that if God wanted me to have a suit He would lead someone else to buy one for me. The Bible says in Matthew 6:28 "take no thought for raiment for He would provide it in due season if I trusted in Him." Around a week after our conversation took place a godly man asked if he could speak to me after the service. He took me to his van and pulled out a beautiful blue suit and said I hope it fits. He went on to say that the Lord smote his heart and told him to buy it for me. That suit was very nice and I wore it for ten years. Matthews 6:33 says it like this, "Seek ye first the kingdom of God and his righteousness and all these other things will be added unto you." It was a great feeling that night to take off my old used worn out coat and slip on that beautiful new one. Philippians 4:19 says "But my God shall supply all your need according to His riches in glory by Christ Jesus." Blessings from God never get old, but only newer and newer the more you tell them. Thank God for salvation, and how He cleans us up through the blood of His precious Son.

Chapter 11

A Blissful Moment in Time

Nothing in this world thrills and excites me more than reading about great men and women who changed the landscape of their generation through faith. When I read history I marvel at the dedication and effort that people made to make this world a better place.

Billy Sunday preached daily and fought the Devil constantly and saw around one million saved. Charles Spurgeon read 6 books a week, preached 10 times a week wrote 140 books, preached to 10 million, and personally answered around 500 letters a week. Fanny Crosby wrote around 500 songs a year for about 40 straight years. History is filled with such people who were instrumental in changing the world for the kingdom of God.

In the following story I will tell you about a miracle that happened as I was studying about a great man named Phillip Bliss. As I express to you this story think of how rare this story really is and let's give glory to the matchless name of Jesus. I sure hope you enjoy this story.

One night around 5 years ago I was sitting in my chair reading about a songwriter named Phillip Bliss. As I was reading the Holy Spirit was turning me inside out and tears were streaming down my face. Phillip Bliss was responsible for penning some of the greatest hymns ever written and he was totally surrendered to Christ. D.L. Moody once said. "Mr. Bliss was the most talented man he ever met but yet the most humble as well. Another man said, "He never seen Mr. Bliss in public without a smile and a glow." I remember reading for hours that night and feeling weak from weeping.

The very next night we had Wednesday evening service and my dear pastor Timothy Ammon wanted to speak to me after services. After the preaching concluded we went into his office and talked for a minute. Pastor Ammon then gave me a package and said, "This is a book just for you. Tony for many years, people have tried to get this book from me but I didn't have peace about giving it away but now I do, please enjoy it." Pastor closed by saying, "Open it in your car." I said, "Sure."

When I opened my car I sat down and began to unwrap it. As I read the title I could not believe my eyes. The book was entitled, "The life and times of Phillip Bliss" and it was from the 1800's. As I gazed on that book God's power fell on me for around 30 minutes. Folks that is beyond rare; AMEN. Two years later I felt a need to reach out to a young man who was hungry for God. My mindset that day was to feed him as much hymn history as possible and some how I got around to sharing with him the history of Phillip Bliss. The very next day something outstanding took place. While working in Detroit I received a long text from the same young man I talked with the day before. He said, "Tony, are you sitting down?" I responded, "Yes Sir." He proceeded to tell a story that was hard to believe. He said, "Tony, as I was working at Wal-Mart this morning I heard a voice over the loud speaker that said Phillip Bliss report to the front." He said, "I ran up to the front to see if I could catch him but no one was there."

The day before we talked about Phillip Bliss who lived in the 1800's and the next day that exact name blasted over the loud speaker so everyone could hear that wonderful name.

I'm grateful for God's amazing kindness. He is such a great Savior

Chapter 12

Hiding Under the Shadows of the Almighty

As I grow older in the Lord I find myself somewhere in the book of Psalms every day. The book of Psalms covers every aspect of life and its pages refresh me daily. Many great Christian's today run to the book of Psalms whenever danger is near and I must admit I do too. Nearly every verse in this wonderful book will motivate you to serve God at a higher level than you did the day before.

With the rest of this chapter I want to highlight what God can do for those who hide under the shadow of the Almighty. I pray this chapter magnifies the name of our Great God.

A few years ago as I was on the internet listening to music I heard that the Talley's were going to be in my area singing for God's glory. I've always liked the Talley's songs and their family has a rich history of honoring the Lord so I quickly bought two tickets for my dad and me. All throughout the day of the concert God directed me to Psalms 91 and He would not give me peace about reading anything else that day. As we arrived at the church to hear the singing God swept over my soul that night. My main desire, that night, was to hear the singing, meet the Talley's and give them a signed book. When the concert was over people flooded their table so I stayed behind and read Psalms 91:4 over and over again. A great peace filled my heart as I read that great verse for the final time. Once the reading was over I walked up to the Talley's CD table and we talked for a minute. Mrs. Debra Talley stopped in mid sentence and said I have something for you to have sir; wait a second. Mrs. Talley then came back with a book and said I am going to sign my favorite verse in here for you. She grabbed the writer's pen and wrote down Psalms 91:4 and smiled at me. Folks it is not by accident she signed that verse for that is the exact verse God directed me to all day.

When we abide under his wings we will always be better for it. Trust God, do what He says, for His power is great and His understanding is infinite. Life is very simple get out of the way and let Jesus lead the why. Abide under the shadows of the Almighty and God will help you all your days.

Chapter 13

All Things Are Possible With God

Never allow negative hurtful people to rob you of your dreams. There are folks all over the world that will cast doubt and gloom on our visions and dreams and the best thing we can do is eliminate those people from our lives. The older I'm getting the more I'm surrounding myself with folks that truly share in my visions and will support me instead of drain me. Always remember as long as Joseph was around his jealous family his life never took off for God's glory. When he got away from these bad influences he soared with God and became second in command in the land of Egypt.

All the great business people of this world warn against listening to bad advice and as Christians we need to heed the same advice. I don't care how long someone has been going to church if they offer no support and bad advice I'm junking it because it will harm me later down the road. The Bible says that we ought to obey God rather than man. Believe in yourself and trust that God can do anything whether others think so or not. With God anything is possible and these events that follow will prove just that.

    I woke up one Saturday morning and I could not get a gospel singing group from Tennessee out of my mind. The group that was on my mind was a famous group called Legacy Five. The Lord laid it heavy on my heart that morning to get them my book, "Walking on the water with Jesus" as soon as possible. My first thought was to send a book to their address but God quickly changed my mind and I dropped to my knees in prayer. My prayer to God was simply this, "Lord please allow this book to make it to the Legacy Five safe and sound. Thank you Lord, amen." After my prayer had ended I noticed that I had received a picture and it was from my dear wife. My wife was stopped by a red light and she looked over and right next to her was the Legacy Five tour bus and she took a picture. When she sent the picture it happened to be just minutes from where we lived. Legacy Five was performing just miles up the road so I went to take them my book. Before I got out of the car I asked the Lord to make it easy and God answered my prayer. I opened my car door and just a matter of steps away, was Scott Fowler, lead singer of Legacy Five and I handed him the book.

    Months later God laid it on my heart to get a book to Mr. Jason Crabb which was not an easy feat. I found out that my dear friend Brad Ledbetter was singing at the National Quartet Convention and that Jason Crabb would be there as well. Mr. Crabb is one of the most famous singers in America and the odds of getting a book to him were nearly impossible but my friend agreed to try. At the National Quartet Convention there are thousands of people and hundreds of singers. For the next few days I prayed about this situation and after two days I received a message from my friend and it was amazing news. Brad Ledbetter said, "Tony, you won't believe this but they put Jason Crabb's booth right next to mine so I can get him your book." My response was, "oh I believe it brother because prayers work." We both gave God the glory for what he did that day.

Around 6 months later as I was teaching my teen class I made the statement that my next goal was to get my book to Mr. Bill Gaither. After making this statement a teen shouted out, "You will never get it to him. He is the most famous song writer in the world." I quickly told the young man never to make that statement and that God would answer this prayer through faith.

A few months later Gaither tickets became available to me and I told my mom this is ordained of God and I ordered two tickets to see Bill Gaither. All throughout the day of that concert I told my mother we are going for a reason; trust me God will make it easy. Normally the Gaithers pack out arenas easily but on this night they had a low turnout. My mother sat back in amazement as I walked directly up to all the Gaither members and gave them my book. Nothing is impossible with God and this last story will be a final stamp of authority on this subject.

Many experts will agree that the hardest challenge in the world today is for a common man to get an opportunity to speak to the president, or presidential candidates. Many people laughed when I told them that by the end of the year I would get my book to Mr. Ted Cruz. Folks, no one is laughing now. In three short months after making this statement God raised up three people who I never met to personally hand my book to Mr. Ted Cruz. The odds of this happening were off the charts and I still praise God for what He did in all these different events.

The moral of this story is simple. Don't allow others to

control your; life rather allow God's Spirit to. Soar with God, without the permission of others. All my life people have hurt me, tried to stop me, and cast doubt on what I'm doing but the less I listen to that noise the more I attain joy. Always remember people called Einstein and Edison stupid when they were young but history records they changed the world through their wisdom. The great book, "The Cat in the Hat," was rejected 27 times before a publisher accepted it. Before Mr. Seuss died millions upon millions were sold.

People will always rise up to stop you when you go to make a difference. My advice, kill them with kindness and go on for the glory of God. Jude 22 "And of some have compassion making a difference."

Chapter 14

RED AND YELLOW; BLACK AND WHITE; THEY'RE ALL PRECIOUS IN HIS SIGHT

There was a song I learned as a little boy that spoke volumes to my soul concerning the mind of God. The song is titled, "Jesus loves the little children of the world." Within this little song was a phrase that opened up God's mind and God's heart to me at a very young age. The phrase reads like this, "Red and yellow; black and white; they're all precious in His sight." Jesus died for all the children of the world. Once I allowed this song to sink into my heart I realized that God is not a racist nor does He prejudge anyone. No! God is loving and caring. Jesus wants the best for each of us. Many do not see this. Most people that I've come across allow Satan to convince them that anytime something goes wrong it is God's fault. Always remember Jesus willingly died for the sins of the world and Satan is the great deceiver. If the Devil can get people to believe this he will take their hope, their strength, and eventually their life.

Statistics say that around 80% of what people say or do is negative in its nature. The Devil has folks confused and defeated before they even make it out of their bed each morning. There is a spiritual battle that rages daily and it takes place between our ears. God wants your mind according to Philippians 2:5 and Satan wants it as well according to II Corinthians 4:4 . How our lives turn out is totally dependent on who we allow to control our minds. We must train ourselves to think positive and Godly in this present evil world. If we don't we are no match for the Devil. No matter what your problems are, the answer is found in a great God who cares for you whether you believe it or not.

This next story proves to the world that through prayer anything is obtainable. Allow God to encourage you with this following story.

Every day of my life I rub shoulders with folks that willingly tell me about their many problems. It amazes me what some go through and it breaks my heart. People are giving up on life and depression is claiming thousands every year. All I can do as a man of God is offer hope through a man named Jesus Christ. Some will receive it and some will reject it but my job is to reach out with a loving heart. One day a man approached me and his list of problems were longer than anyone I've ever met. Every day he carried bitterness and unforgiveness around with him and I could see the pain on his face. This man has always been kind to me but if anyone brought up God he would curse and scream. One day he asked me if I wanted a pop and for some reason it touched my heart and I said, "Sure my friend and thank you." I remember looking at him and saying, "Sir I will pray that God shows compassion on you tonight for helping me just now. He looked at me and said ," Tony, all my life it has been a train wreak and I do not believe in God like you do." I turned to him and said," We will talk tomorrow, let me know what happens." The very next day he came to me with joy and told me a wonderful story that thrilled my soul.

He said," Tony, as I was walking up my driveway today towards my house I looked and there was $40 staring back at me." He said," Tony that was the first time in my life something good has happened to me." I said, "Randy, God did that for you to prove that He loves and cares for you," Randy walked away smiling while holding that $40 in his hands.

If we let go of our bitterness and look towards the Son things will always become brighter on our pathway. Let me close with this verse in Psalms 16:11 that says, " Thou wilt shew me the path of life: in thy presence is fulness of joy; at thy right hand there are pleasures for evermore.

Chapter 15

The Importance of Waiting on God

Every single day of my life I try to stress the importance of waiting on God in every decision we make. There are literally hundreds of verses about being patient and waiting for the guidance of a loving Savior. In my 35 years in church I've sadly watched teenager after teenager gather many scars and regrets through quick decisions made without God's help. Even sadder is the large number of adults I've known who have found themselves in a world of hurt because they tried to outrun God instead of listening to His Spirit.

Proverbs 14:12 teaches that, "There is a way which seemeth right unto a man, but the end there of are the ways of death."

Never trust your feelings, flesh and emotions over God's Word which never fails. Feelings and emotions change daily but for 6,000 years God's Word has never changed. Every decision we make needs to be ordered by the Lord. With God's leadership we will find peace and rest. Anything outside of this will result in ruin and it will be as sinking sand. Psalm

46:10 has helped me more often than any verse in God's holy Word when it comes to waiting on God. In nearly every Bible bookstore in this country you will find this phrase, "be still and know that I am God."

I hope and pray that this following story will stress the importance of waiting on God in our everyday life.

Not long ago my dear wife came to me and asked if we could look for a 42 inch flat screen TV. It had been a while since we got anything for ourselves so I said sure lets go take a look. We got in the car and traveled 20 minutes to a store and looked at all their TV's. As we were looking I began to feel a sense of peace. I told my wife that tonight is not the night, lets wait a few weeks. We went home that night obeying the voice of God and not our flesh and God was pleased. About 2 weeks later we received a call from a dear friend and the news was glorious. The women on the other line said to my wife, "Erin, do you need a 42 inch flat screen TV? I've only used it a few times." We quickly said "yes, we would." Not only did God reward us for waiting, He gave us exactly the same TV we were looking at a few weeks earlier at the store.

We will have a greater sense of joy and peace if we learn to wait on God. If we learn this simple principle of God life will be much more enjoyable. Thank God's for his sweet Holy Spirit in our lives. I do not want to ever be in a hurry while serving God however I want to be in a position where I can hear his still small voice at any time wherever I am. Many miss his voice because they attempt to out run the Lord. That is always a mistake in whatever decision we make. Waiting on God is so important and I hope many have learned this truth through reading this simple chapter.

Chapter 16

Jesus Knows Exactly What He's Doing

Sometimes things happen that shock us. Circumstances get out of our control. Jesus, according to His Word, is the King of Kings and Lord of Lords and He is exactly what we need when times get rough. We will never understand why friends and family die suddenly, but we must understand that there is a reason for everything that takes place. Sometimes things happen to grab our attention and cause us to think about eternity. Hebrews 9:27 still teaches that there is an appointment with death that we all must keep. Heaven and hell are very real and we must prepare to meet our God. Many times in order to get one's attention He causes hardships and tragedy to unfold so that we will look up and seek the salvation we so desperately need. Nothing happens by accident and everything happens by design. If life always went good we would never think about eternity and we would die suddenly and wake up in a darkened hell. With love divine He tries in every way to get you to think about your final state when you leave this life.

This story proves that God understands your situation and He will gladly be there if you will invite Him in. Allow me to help you with this story.

One day at work a man I'm very close to received word that his cousin sadly passed away in a tragic motorcycle accident at a very young age. My heart broke for this man and I wondered what I could do to help. As the day went on something within me told me to give him one verse in the Bible -- Matthew 11:28. This is a famous verse in the Bible which says, "Come unto me, all ye that labor and are heavy laden and I will give you rest," That night he went home and couldn't sleep and read this verse over and over again. Never before that day had he taken a liking to the Bible but God got a hold of his heart. The next morning he approached me and said you picked a good verse and I want you to know that I read it over and over again. I said I'm proud of you and I'm glad you read that verse. After our conversation I had to go on the road to Detroit to pick up equipment. All through the day I was praying for this man and Matthew 11:28 kept running through my mind. As we neared the close of the day and we threw the last sign on our truck I noticed a huge church to my right. Next to the church was a big sign with a verse attached to it. Out of all the verses in the Bible that it could have been it happened to be Matthew 11:28, "Come unto me all ye that labor and are heavy laden and I will give you rest."

You see, my friend God knows what He is doing. God sends so many warnings throughout our lives to cause us to look to His cross where He paid the price for us. We try our best to ignore Him, but we are only lying to ourselves. All you have to do is run to Christ and He will give you rest. One day life will end, and eternity will begin. Stop running away from the Lord, but rather look and live my brother live. Just think about it, without this tragedy in this man's life he may have never read that verse. God wants to rescue you today if you will only give Him a chance.

Chapter 17

Surely Goodness and Mercy Shall Follow Me All the Days of My Life

All young people at a very early age need to read Psalms 23:6. This verse without a doubt can change the course of a young person's life if it is understood and followed. Psalms 23:6 reads like this, "surely goodness and mercy shall follow me all the days of my life: and I will dwell in the house of the Lord forever.

Faithfulness according to God's Word is the greatest thing a person can have and without it blessings from God will disappear. If a person is inconsistent in the things of the Lord they will struggle all the days of their life.

As a very young man I had a desire to have the blessings of God in my life so I tithed on every check and was at church every service. I'm 35 years old now and I have never regretted that decision. Day after day God sends His goodness my way and it's all because I've been faithful toward the things of

God.

God made a promise in Psalms 23:6 that will never fade away but it's up to us to obey His Word and reap the benefits. Let me give you this story to prove that this verse is true.

A few years back God told me to teach on the subject, "Surely goodness and mercy shall follow me all the days of my life." My goal in teaching that morning was to drive home the point that God has special blessings for those who serve Him. That morning alone we used around 75 verses and 10 stories proving this was true and God was really moving on their young hearts. At the close of the class I told the kids that every day something special happens for our family because we love God and want to be faithful to Him.

Hours later after this statement my mother said someone dropped off a gift with my name on it. I remember opening the package and inside was 96 Reese peanut butter cups. Instantly my mind went back to the message I taught that day and joy filled my soul.

Let me close this chapter by saying this, "many want blessings in their lives but when you mention faithfulness it stops them cold in their tracks." If you will be faithful to God then God will be faithful to you. Serve God all your days and you will never regret it. Give him every corner of your heart and the results will be overwhelming.

Chapter 18

Love Conquers Al

All Christians around this country need to take the time, once a week, to read 1 Corinthians chapter 13. Paul, under the inspiration of the Holy Spirit, tells us over and over that if we live our lives without love we are really not living at all. Paul made this statement in 1 Corinthians 13:2, "And though I have all faith, so that I could remove mountains and have not charity, I am nothing.

Far too many Christians try to function without love and as a consequence they live as spiritually dead people, causing dead churches.

Pastors all around this country preach hard and pound on the pulpit and people go out of their services worse than they came in because love is not flowing through the services. Any man of God that makes a difference will have a balance of doctrine and love. To have one without the other is a false balance and proverbs 11:1 says that a false balance is an abomination unto the Lord. Without a steady dose of love a church will crumble.

If this is true in a church that is ordained by God it is

also true in a biblical marriage that is also ordained by God. Matthew 19:6 says, "Wherefore they are no more twain but one flesh. What God hath joined together, let no man put asunder." God has always intended for all marriages to thrive and last forever but sadly many fall apart because love vanishes from the marriage. Even God had to give His people a bill of divorce because they were backslidden and lost their love for Him and cheated on Him. When love is present in a marriage all things are possible. However if it leaves it will quickly become impossible.

A relationship is dictated by how much love dwells within a home. God has always intended for marriage to last forever and I hope this story proves the second part of Matthew 19:6, "What God hath joined together let no man put sunder.

Around a year ago my wedding ring came up missing and I had no earthly idea where it was. After a day of looking for it I told my wife that I had misplaced it. We were scheduled to go to Hillsdale, Michigan that week so we went and never looked back. I assured my wife that once we got back from Hillsdale I would find it and I didn't want her to worry. We spent three great days in Hillsdale and we arrived back home on a Sunday night. After we unpacked from our trip I made a point to look everywhere for that ring but I could not find it. The very next morning, before I left for work, I made one final attempt to find the ring but I could not find it. I worked a full shift that day and on my way home something amazing happened. Songs of love and assurance rapidly flowed through my mind and a peace flooded my soul. Somehow and someway I just knew my ring was safe and sound and the remainder of my drive was pleasant. I remember pulling in my yard and thanking God for keeping my ring safe. As I opened the door I looked on the grass and without taking a step I reached down and picked up my ring like nothing ever happened.

    Three months later after playing basketball my ring came up missing again. For over 4 months I could not find my ring. Never during that time did I worry or stress over it because I knew God would keep it safe. Sure enough, as I was listening to gospel music one day I looked down and in between the seats of my car my ring was looking back at me. What's amazing about this is that I found it on our 7th year anniversary. Romans 8:38-9 is so powerful when you read these verses in its entirety. Romans 8: 38-39 says, "For I am persuaded that neither death, nor life, nor angels, nor principalities, nor powers, nor things present, nor things to come, nor heights, nor depths, nor any other creature shall be able to separate us from the love of God, which is in Christ Jesus our Lord.

CONCLUSION

    As we conclude this book I hope something within these pages motivated you to serve God better in these last days. We all understand that as the rapture approaches the fiery darts of the wicked will only increase. It's not good enough to be just a lukewarm Christian in these last days. We need people on fire for God. This generation of people is going to hell, at a record pace, and it is because we as Christians have lost our power with God. Soaring with Eagles is meant to infuse life back into those who have grown weary from the battle. Christians are dropping like flies, backsliding, and falling by the wayside in record numbers. Many who do come look like death warmed over. Oh how we need life and liberty back in our churches. We always heard the statement that says, "as goes our churches so goes the nation" As long as the power of God is missing from our churches, people as a whole, will grew darker in their hearts around this great nation. When the fire of God returns in people's hearts again we will see amazing results. However if it does not return then revival is hopeless. Life is too short and God is too good for us to live a half hearted Christian life.

    Jesus deserves our very best and I pray God's Spirit has refreshed you as you read this book. I pray that we will take an examination of our lives and ask ourselves are we closer to

God right now than we were yesterday. If the answer is no then we need to ask God to renew us like the eagles for His honor and glory. My prayer is that this book will affect millions in the years to come and that revival fires will spread through this feeble effort. Thank God for his Power that is available to us. We must hunger and long after it.

    With Love
    Brother Tony
    Isaiah 40:31

BUILDING BLOCKS THAT WILL LEAD YOU TO GOD'S POWER

Before completely closing out this book I feel led by the Lord to give you some building blocks from God's Word that will lead you to God's power in your life. God's power is not for a chosen few like so many believe but it is for any child of God who wants it from the depths of their soul. If you wish to soar with God it will not be easy but I will give you the recipe for success from God's holy book. We will discuss 15 words from the Bible that will lift any Christian to new heights with God if they are followed and added to people's lives. The fifteen words are joy, strength, power, peace, giving, soul winning, prayer, wisdom, love, faithfulness, compassion, studying, patience, singing and faith. We will write out each word and give verses along with each word. If you add these verses to your life I promise you will be soaring with eagles soon. The verses I will give you have always helped me and I know they will help you as well. Read each verse carefully. Add these words to your life and you will be amazed at where you will be with God a year from now. I hope these verses help you see the importance of getting close to the lord and winning battles in your own personal life.

ADD COMPASSION TO YOUR LIFE

Jude 1:22 And of some have compassion, making a difference:

Matthew 15:32 Then Jesus called his disciples unto him, and said, I have compassion on the multitude, because they continue with me now three days, and have nothing to eat: and I will not send them away fasting, lest they faint in the way.

\Luke 15:20 And he arose, and came to his father. But when he was yet a great way off, his father saw him, and had compassion, and ran, and fell on his neck, and kissed him.

Matthew 9:36 But when he saw the multitudes, he was moved with compassion on them, because they fainted, and were scattered abroad, as sheep having no shepherd.

Mark 1:41 And Jesus, moved with compassion, put forth his hand, and touched him, and saith unto him, I will; be thou clean.

1Peter 3:8 Finally, be ye all of one mind, having compassion one of another, love as brethren, be pitiful, be courteous:

1John 3:17 But whoso hath this world's good, and seeth his brother have need, and shutteth up his bowels of compassion from him, how dwelleth the love of God in him?

Psalm 78:38 But he, being full of compassion, forgave their iniquity, and destroyed them not: yea, many a time turned he his anger away, and did not stir up all his wrath.

Psalm 86:15 But thou, O Lord, art a God full of compassion, and gracious, longsuffering, and plenteous in mercy and truth.

Psalm 145:8 The LORD is gracious, and full of compassion; slow to anger, and of great mercy.

ADD FAITH TO YOUR LIFE

Hebrews 11:1 Now faith is the substance of things hoped for, the evidence of things not seen.

Hebrews 11:6 But without faith it is impossible to please him: for he that cometh to God must believe that he is, and that he is a rewarder of them that diligently seek him.

Matthew 15:28 Then Jesus answered and said unto her, O woman, great is thy faith: be it unto thee even as thou wilt. And her daughter was made whole from that very hour.

Matthew 8:10 When Jesus heard it, he marvelled, and said to them that followed, Verily I say unto you, I have not found so great faith, no, not in Israel.

Matthew 17:20 And Jesus said unto them, Because of your unbelief: for verily I say unto you, If ye have faith as a grain of mustard seed, ye shall say unto this mountain, Remove hence to yonder place; and it shall remove; and nothing shall be impossible unto you.

Romans 10:17 So then faith cometh by hearing, and hearing by the Word of God.

James 1:6 But let him ask in faith, nothing wavering. For he that wavereth is like a wave of the sea driven with the wind and tossed.

2Peter 1:1 Simon Peter, a servant and an apostle of Jesus Christ, to them that have obtained like precious faith with us through the righteousness of God and our Saviour Jesus Christ:

1Peter 1:7 That the trial of your faith, being much more precious than of gold that perisheth, though it be tried with fire, might be found unto praise and honour and glory at the appearing of Jesus Christ:

James 2:5 Hearken, my beloved brethren, Hath not God chosen the poor of this world rich in faith, and heirs of the kingdom which he hath promised to them that love him?

ADD FAITHFULNESS TO YOUR LIFE

Hebrews 10:25 Not forsaking the assembling of ourselves together, as the manner of some is; but exhorting one another: and so much the more, as ye see the day approaching.

Psalm 84:10 For a day in thy courts is better than a thousand. I had rather be a doorkeeper in the house of my God, than to dwell in the tents of wickedness.

Psalm 27:4 One thing have I desired of the LORD, that will I seek after; that I may dwell in the house of the LORD all the days of my life, to behold the beauty of the LORD, and to enquire in his temple.

Psalm 23:6 Surely goodness and mercy shall follow me all the days of my life: and I will dwell in the house of the LORD for ever.

Psalm 100:4 Enter into his gates with thanksgiving, and into his courts with praise: be thankful unto him, and bless his name.

1Corinthians 4:2 Moreover it is required in stewards, that a man be found faithful.

Psalm 122:1 A Song of degrees of David. I was glad when they said unto me, Let us go into the house of the LORD.

Mark 12:30 And thou shalt love the Lord thy God with all thy heart, and with all thy soul, and with all thy mind, and with all thy strength: this is the first commandment.

Romans 12:1 I beseech you therefore, brethren, by the mercies of God, that ye present your bodies a living sacrifice, holy, acceptable unto God, which is your reasonable service.

Joshua 24:15 And if it seem evil unto you to serve the LORD, choose you this day whom ye will serve; whether the gods which your fathers served that were on the other side of the flood, or the gods of the Amorites, in whose land ye dwell: but as for me and my house, we will serve the LORD.

ADD GIVING TO YOUR LIFE

Luke 6:38 Give, and it shall be given unto you; good measure, pressed down, and shaken together, and running over, shall men give into your bosom. For with the same measure that ye mete withal it shall be measured to you again.

Acts 20:35 I have shewed you all things, how that so labouring ye ought to support the weak, and to remember the Words of the Lord Jesus, how he said, It is more blessed to give than to receive.

2Corinthians 9:7 Every man according as he purposeth in his heart, so let him give; not grudgingly, or of necessity: for God loveth a cheerful giver.

Matthew 5:42 Give to him that asketh thee, and from him that would borrow of thee turn not thou away.

Matthew 19:21 Jesus said unto him, If thou wilt be perfect, go and sell that thou hast, and give to the poor, and thou shalt have treasure in heaven: and come and follow me.

Acts 3:6 Then Peter said, Silver and gold have I none; but such as I have give I thee: In the name of Jesus Christ of Nazareth rise up and walk.

John 3:16 For God so loved the world, that he gave his only begotten Son, that whosoever believeth in him should not perish, but have everlasting life.

1John 3:16 Hereby perceive we the love of God, because he laid down his life for us: and we ought to lay down our lives for the brethren.

Romans 8:32 He that spared not his own Son, but delivered him up for us all, how shall he not with him also freely give us all things?

James 1:5 If any of you lack wisdom, let him ask of God, that giveth to all men liberally, and upbraideth not; and it shall be given him.

ADD JOY TO YOUR LIFE

Psalm 16:11 Thou wilt shew me the path of life: in thy presence is fulness of joy; at thy right hand there are pleasures for evermore.

Nehemiah 8:10 Then he said unto them, Go your way, eat the fat, and drink the sweet, and send portions unto them for whom nothing is prepared: for this day is holy unto our Lord: neither be ye sorry; for the joy of the LORD is your strength.

1Peter 1:8 Whom having not seen, ye love; in whom, though now ye see him not, yet believing, ye rejoice with joy unspeakable and full of glory:

Jude 1:24 Now unto him that is able to keep you from falling, and to present you faultless before the presence of his glory with exceeding joy,

1John 1:4 And these things write we unto you, that your joy may be full.

Hebrews 12:2 Looking unto Jesus the author and finisher of our faith; who for the joy that was set before him endured the cross, despising the shame, and is set down at the right hand of the throne of God.

Isaiah 35:10 And the ransomed of the LORD shall return, and come to Zion with songs and everlasting joy upon their heads: they shall obtain joy and gladness, and sorrow and sighing shall flee away.

Psalm 30:5 For his anger endureth but a moment; in his favour is life: weeping may endure for a night, but joy cometh in the morning.

Luke 15:10 Likewise, I say unto you, there is joy in the presence of the angels of God over one sinner that repenteth.

John 15:11 These things have I spoken unto you, that my joy might remain in you, and that your joy might be full.

ADD LOVE TO YOUR LIFE

Proverbs 10:12 Hatred stirreth up strifes: but love covereth all sins.

Jude 1:21 Keep yourselves in the love of God, looking for the mercy of our Lord Jesus Christ unto eternal life.

Romans 13:10 Love worketh no ill to his neighbour: therefore love is the fulfilling of the law.

2Corinthians 13:11 Finally, brethren, farewell. Be perfect, be of good comfort, be of one mind, live in peace; and the God of love and peace shall be with you.

John 15:13 Greater love hath no man than this, that a man lay down his life for his friends.

Ephesians 3:19 And to know the love of Christ, which passeth knowledge, that ye might be filled with all the fulness of God.

2Timothy 1:7 For God hath not given us the spirit of fear; but of power, and of love, and of a sound mind.

Revelation 1:5 And from Jesus Christ, who is the faithful witness, and the first begotten of the dead, and the prince of the kings of the earth. Unto him that loved us, and washed us from our sins in his own blood,

1John 4:8 He that loveth not knoweth not God; for God is love.

John 14:15 If ye love me, keep my commandments.

ADD PATIENCE TO YOUR LIFE

Romans 15:5 Now the God of patience and consolation grant you to be likeminded one toward another according to Christ Jesus:

Romans 5:3 And not only so, but we glory in tribulations also: knowing that tribulation worketh patience;

James 1:3 Knowing this, that the trying of your faith worketh patience.

James 5:11 Behold, we count them happy which endure. Ye have heard of the patience of Job, and have seen the end of the Lord; that the Lord is very pitiful, and of tender mercy.

Titus 2:2 That the aged men be sober, grave, temperate, sound in faith, in charity, in patience.

2Peter 1:6 And to knowledge temperance; and to temperance patience; and to patience godliness;

Hebrews 12:1 Wherefore seeing we also are compassed about with so great a cloud of witnesses, let us lay aside every weight, and the sin which doth so easily beset us, and let us run with patience the race that is set before us,

Revelation 3:10 Because thou hast kept the word of my patience, I also will keep thee from the hour of temptation, which shall come upon all the world, to try them that dwell upon the earth.

Luke 8:15 But that on the good ground are they, which in an honest and good heart, having heard the word, keep it, and bring forth fruit with patience.

2Corinthians 6:4 But in all things approving ourselves as the ministers of God, in much patience, in afflictions, in necessities, in distresses,

ADD PEACE TO YOUR LIFE

Isaiah 26:3 Thou wilt keep him in perfect peace, whose mind is stayed on thee: because he trusteth in thee.

Ephesians 2:14 For he is our peace, who hath made both one, and hath broken down the middle wall of partition between us;

Psalm 34:14 Depart from evil, and do good; seek peace, and pursue it.

Luke 2:14 Glory to God in the highest, and on earth peace, good will toward men.

Romans 1:7 To all that be in Rome, beloved of God, called to be saints: Grace to you and peace from God our Father, and the Lord Jesus Christ.

John 14:27 Peace I leave with you, my peace I give unto you: not as the world giveth, give I unto you. Let not your heart be troubled, neither let it be afraid.

John 16:33 These things I have spoken unto you, that in me ye might have peace. In the world ye shall have tribulation: but be of good cheer; I have overcome the world.

Isaiah 48:18 O that thou hadst hearkened to my commandments! then had thy peace been as a river, and thy righteousness as the waves of the sea:

Colossians 3:15 And let the peace of God rule in your hearts, to the which also ye are called in one body; and be ye thankful.

2Peter 1:2 Grace and peace be multiplied unto you through the knowledge of God, and of Jesus our Lord,

ADD POWER TO YOUR LIFE

Philippians 3:10 That I may know him, and the power of his resurrection, and the fellowship of his sufferings, being made conformable unto his death;

Luke 24:49 And, behold, I send the promise of my Father upon you: but tarry ye in the city of Jerusalem, until ye be endued with power from on high.

2Corinthians 12:9 And he said unto me, My grace is sufficient for thee: for my strength is made perfect in weakness. Most gladly therefore will I rather glory in my infirmities, that the power of Christ may rest upon me.

Ephesians 3:20 Now unto him that is able to do exceeding abundantly above all that we ask or think, according to the power that worketh in us,

Ephesians 1:19 And what is the exceeding greatness of his power to us-ward who believe, according to the working of his mighty power,

Romans 15:13 Now the God of hope fill you with all joy and peace in believing, that ye may abound in hope, through the power of the Holy Ghost.

Genesis 32:28 And he said, Thy name shall be called no more Jacob, but Israel: for as a prince hast thou power with God and with men, and hast prevailed.

Isaiah 40:29 He giveth power to the faint; and to them that have no might he increaseth strength.

Acts 1:8 But ye shall receive power, after that the Holy Ghost is come upon you: and ye shall be witnesses unto me both in Jerusalem, and in all Judaea, and in Samaria, and unto the uttermost part of the earth.

Luke 4:14 And Jesus returned in the power of the Spirit into Galilee: and there went out a fame of him through all the region round about.

ADD PRAYER TO YOUR LIFE

Acts 4:31 And when they had prayed, the place was shaken where they were assembled together; and they were all filled with the Holy Ghost, and they spake the Word of God with boldness.

Jude 1:20 But ye, beloved, building up yourselves on your most holy faith, praying in the Holy Ghost,

1Thessalonians 5:17 Pray without ceasing.

Psalm 34:15 The eyes of the LORD are upon the righteous, and his ears are open unto their cry.

Jeremiah 33:3 Call unto me, and I will answer thee, and shew thee great and mighty things, which thou knowest not.

James 5:16 Confess your faults one to another, and pray one for another, that ye may be healed. The effectual fervent prayer of a righteous man availeth much.

Daniel 6:10 Now when Daniel knew that the writing was signed, he went into his house; and his windows being open in his chamber toward Jerusalem, he kneeled upon his knees three times a day, and prayed, and gave thanks before his God, as he did aforetime.

Psalm 55:17 Evening, and morning, and at noon, will I pray, and cry aloud: and he shall hear my voice.

Psalm 5:3 My voice shalt thou hear in the morning, O LORD; in the morning will I direct my prayer unto thee, and will look up.

Acts 9:40 But Peter put them all forth, and kneeled down, and prayed; and turning him to the body said, Tabitha, arise. And she opened her eyes; and when she saw Peter, she sat up.

ADD SINGING TO YOUR LIFE

Ephesians 5:19 Speaking to yourselves in psalms and hymns and spiritual songs, singing and making melody in your heart to the Lord;

Colossians 3:16 Let the word of Christ dwell in you richly in all wisdom; teaching and admonishing one another in psalms and hymns and spiritual songs, singing with grace in your hearts to the Lord.

Psalm 100:2 Serve the LORD with gladness: come before his presence with singing.

Psalm 126:2 Then was our mouth filled with laughter, and our tongue with singing: then said they among the heathen, The LORD hath done great things for them.

Revelation 5:9 And they sung a new song, saying, Thou art worthy to take the book, and to open the seals thereof: for thou wast slain, and hast redeemed us to God by thy blood out of every kindred, and tongue, and people, and nation;

Psalm 40:3 And he hath put a new song in my mouth, even praise unto our God: many shall see it, and fear, and shall trust in the LORD.

Psalm 18:49 Therefore will I give thanks unto thee, O LORD, among the heathen, and sing praises unto thy name.

Psalm 30:4 Sing unto the LORD, O ye saints of his, and give thanks at the remembrance of his holiness.

Psalm 138:5 Yea, they shall sing in the ways of the LORD: for great is the glory of the LORD.

Song of Solomon 2:12 The flowers appear on the earth; the time of the singing of birds is come, and the voice of the turtle is heard in our land;

ADD SOUL WINNING TO YOUR LIFE

Matthew 4:19 And he saith unto them, Follow me, and I will make you fishers of men.

Mark 16:15 And he said unto them, Go ye into all the world, and preach the gospel to every creature.

Luke 14:23 And the lord said unto the servant, Go out into the highways and hedges, and compel them to come in, that my house may be filled.

Psalm 126:6 He that goeth forth and weepeth, bearing precious seed, shall doubtless come again with rejoicing, bringing his sheaves with him.

Acts 20:26 Wherefore I take you to record this day, that I am pure from the blood of all men.

Matthew 6:20 But lay up for yourselves treasures in heaven, where neither moth nor rust doth corrupt, and where thieves do not break through nor steal:

Luke 19:10 For the Son of man is come to seek and to save that which was lost.

Matthew 28:19 Go ye therefore, and teach all nations, baptizing them in the name of the Father, and of the Son, and of the Holy Ghost:

Mark 5:20 And he departed, and began to publish in Decapolis how great things Jesus had done for him: and all men did marvel.

Romans 10:1 Brethren, my heart's desire and prayer for Israel is, that they might be saved.

ADD STRENGTH TO YOUR LIFE

Ephesians 6:10 Finally, my brethren, be strong in the Lord, and in the power of his might.

Philippians 4:13 I can do all things through Christ which strengtheneth me.

Psalm 18:32 It is God that girdeth me with strength, and maketh my way perfect.

Psalm 27:1 A Psalm of David. The LORD is my light and my salvation; whom shall I fear? the LORD is the strength of my life; of whom shall I be afraid?

Exodus 15:2 The LORD is my strength and song, and he is become my salvation: he is my God, and I will prepare him an habitation; my father's God, and I will exalt him.

2Samuel 22:33 God is my strength and power: and he maketh my way perfect.

Proverbs 10:29 The way of the LORD is strength to the upright: but destruction shall be to the workers of iniquity

Isaiah 12:2 Behold, God is my salvation; I will trust, and not be afraid: for the LORD JEHOVAH is my strength and my song; he also is become my salvation.

Psalm 29:11 The LORD will give strength unto his people; the LORD will bless his people with peace.

Psalm 46:1 To the chief Musician for the sons of Korah, A Song upon Alamoth. God is our refuge and strength, a very present help in trouble.

ADD STUDYING TO YOUR LIFE

1Timothy 4:13 Till I come, give attendance to reading, to exhortation, to doctrine.

2Timothy 2:15 Study to shew thyself approved unto God, a workman that needeth not to be ashamed, rightly dividing the word of truth.

Acts 17:11 These were more noble than those in Thessalonica, in that they received the word with all readiness of mind, and searched the scriptures daily, whether those things were so.

John 5:39 Search the scriptures; for in them ye think ye have eternal life: and they are they which testify of me.

Hebrews 4:12 For the word of God is quick, and powerful, and sharper than any twoedged sword, piercing even to the dividing asunder of soul and spirit, and of the joints and marrow, and is a discerner of the thoughts and intents of the heart.

Psalm 104:34 My meditation of him shall be sweet: I will be glad in the LORD.

Job 23:12 Neither have I gone back from the commandment of his lips; I have esteemed the words of his mouth more than my necessary food.

Psalm 119:105 NUN. Thy word is a lamp unto my feet, and a light unto my path.

Psalm 119:11 Thy word have I hid in mine heart, that I might not sin against thee.

Psalm 119:133 Order my steps in thy word: and let not any iniquity have dominion over me.

ADD WISDOM TO YOUR LIFE

Proverbs 1:7 The fear of the LORD is the beginning of knowledge: but fools despise wisdom and instruction.

Acts 6:10 And they were not able to resist the wisdom and the spirit by which he spake.

Luke 2:52 And Jesus increased in wisdom and stature, and in favour with God and man.

Proverbs 3:13 Happy is the man that findeth wisdom, and the man that getteth understanding.

Proverbs 4:7 Wisdom is the principal thing; therefore get wisdom: and with all thy getting get understanding.

Revelation 5:12 Saying with a loud voice, Worthy is the Lamb that was slain to receive power, and riches, and wisdom, and strength, and honour, and glory, and blessing.

Daniel 1:20 And in all matters of wisdom and understanding, that the king enquired of them, he found them ten times better than all the magicians and astrologers that were in all his realm.

Proverbs 16:16 How much better is it to get wisdom than gold! and to get understanding rather to be chosen than silver!

Proverbs 8:11 For wisdom is better than rubies; and all the things that may be desired are not to be compared to it.

Proverbs 9:10 The fear of the LORD is the beginning of wisdom: and the knowledge of the holy is understanding.

ANTHONY RITTHALER

Published By Parables

OUR MISSION

The primary mission of Published By Parables, a Christian publisher, is to publish Contemporary and Classic Christian books from an evangelical perspective that honors Christ and promotes the values and virtues of His Kingdom.

Are You An Aspiring Christian Author?

We fulfill our mission best by providing Christian authors and writers publishing options that are uniquely Christian, quick, affordable and easy to understand -- in an effort to please Christ who has called us to a writing ministry. We know the challenges of getting published, especially if you're a first-time author. God, who called you to write your book, will provide the grace sufficient to the task of getting it published.

We understand the value of a dollar; know the importance of producing a quality product; and publish what we publish for the glory of God.

Surf and Explore our site --
then use our easy-to-use "Tell Us" button
to tell us about yourself and about your book.

We're a one-stop, full-service Christian publisher.
We know our limits. We know our capabilities.
You won't be disappointed.

www.PublishedByParables.com

PUBLISHED by PARABLES
Earthly Stories with a Heavenly Meaning